CW00591885

How to write your first book:

Write and publish the book you've
always dreamed of in one month
or less as a beginner

by Isabella G

TABLE OF CONTENTS

INTRODUCTION

Writing a book is no easy task, but trying to do it without guidance is almost impossible as a beginner, not to say time consuming. You don't need to be a professional writer in order to publish a book, as long as you have something to say that's worth saying then I say go for it. With this book on how to write books I will help you with some techniques that have helped me write and publish over 10 books in one year. Everything I wish I knew before starting writing and publishing my own books will be included in full detail in order to help you out as much as I can. For example, this book was written in 15 days. I like tight deadlines because it stress-tests our limits and helps us find our best versions. If this is not your way of operating, I also included other ways to finish a book as well as help with the publishing process.

I'm sure that you're a busy individual who values his or her time, therefore this book is focused on teaching you as much helpful information as possible in the least amount of pages. I'm going to cut out the fluff and leave as much juicy meat for you to consume fast. This way, you can start writing your own book this month without wasting any time trying to figure out how to do it. If you want a 100,000 word book on how to write and publish then this is not for you but if you're into efficiency and getting things done then you've come to the right place.

Throughout the book there will be tips and techniques I've used myself and seen other successful writers use themselves. Keep in mind that what works for me might not work for you and vice versa. I can give you all the tools you need but nothing will work unless you do. It might feel frustrating at first because you'll want to try many different styles but this book and what I'm planning to teach you goes beyond that and it is probably going to be more valuable than just learning how to write a book. I will teach you how to get to know yourself.

****LEGAL DISCLAIMER: The author does not take responsibility for any of the results you might get whether they are derived directly or indirectly from taking any or all of the advice in this book. Likewise, the author will not be responsible for any loss or risk you take. Results and conditions may vary and there is no guarantee you will get the results you want even if you follow every step.

HOW TO WRITE A BOOK

Usually when I tell people that I'm a writer they tell me that they've always wanted to write a book but that they could never do it because it is too ____ (hard, time consuming), or that they're too ____(lazy, disorganized, inconsistent). Whatever excuse you choose to use as the reason you've never written the book you've always wanted to write is just that: an excuse.

Think about where you would be right now if you had taken that first step towards writing a few months ago. If you just thought you'd be on page two I highly doubt it. You'd most likely have a book ready by now! Yes, it might suck and it could be horribly written but you would have something to work with. Bad material is a lot better than no material at all as there's always a way to fix it. Or it could turn out to be a masterpiece and an international best seller! The worst case scenario is that you write it and it ends up selling 3 copies out of which the ones that your mom ordered ended up "getting lost". Even in this case, you end up gaining experience you didn't have before publishing. Think of it this way, even if you only sell 3 copies then that probably means you made your first dollar online anyway. Personally, making my first dollar from a book was the initial step that reassured me that I had found something worth pursuing.

When it comes to the people around you, some of them might support you but most of them will doubt you're going to write a book by yourself. Why listen to them if that's the case? If you know you're capable of writing a book then it is because you are! Don't listen to the critics as this is your road for you to travel, not theirs.

Having said that, I will also add that writing a book is not easy, but it is one of the most rewarding feelings to finish a book you've been working on consistently for a while. You also get that confidence boost from doing what you said you were going to do... a project you've had in the back of your head for years. So, if you are ready to start writing your book and put all the excuses aside, continue reading as I'm going to give you strategies and tips that I use and you can use to finally start, finish and publish your first book.

There isn't one answer that can tell you exactly how to write a book. We are all unique, which means some people might need more time than others to write, or they might not be the best at being creative but are extremely consistent and disciplined. Either way, here are the steps you need to take if you plan to write a book.

CHOOSING A TOPIC

The first thing you need to write a book is a topic. What's the book going to be about? You can't start writing if you don't know what you're going to be writing about. Get clear on what your topic is before you start writing so that you don't end up having to cut your book in half.

Here are some questions you need to ask yourself before you decide what to write about:

Is this book going to be fiction or non-fiction?

The length of a non-fiction book is going to be a lot shorter than a fiction one. Your target market is also very different and getting your book in front of them is going to require different efforts. The writing style is also very different as one is telling a story while the other one is usually teaching you something.

Am I writing this book to make money or because I want to write it to feel fulfilled?

In other words, **Why am I writing this book?**

If you're writing a book to make money you first need to confirm there's a market for it and that people are buying similar books or willing to spend money on the information you have to offer.

If you're writing a book because it would be fulfilling or because it is something you've always wanted to do then it doesn't matter if you only sell one copy as it was more of a challenge to overcome.

Lastly, the reason why you're writing this book will help you keep writing when it becomes hard to stay in front of the computer for another hour typing instead of hanging out with a friend. Your reason why needs to be powerful enough to help you finish your book in one month. It isn't the same to have a powerful reason such as "becoming a best-selling author" than it is to "make $10 extra per month". Remember, this reason is what's going to help you pull through when all other motivation fails.

Have I previously thought about this book or is it a new project?

New projects are usually going to take longer to create as you need to be creative about what's happening, the characters and the storyline. I knew a guy from one of my classes who had been dreaming about writing a book for the longest time, once he actually decided to act on it he ended up with 80,000 words worth of material. Are you familiar with your story? When it comes to non-fiction, this becomes the next question:

Do I know enough about this topic to write a whole book on it?

It's easier to write a book that's set on a city you live in or that you're familiar with than a city that you've never visited or know nothing about.

Likewise, if you plan to write a book on free radicals and you don't even know what that is then you're either headed for trouble or long nights of studying the topic as you'll need to become an expert before you start writing. Writing about what you know could end up being better for yourself as well as for the reader, this is because you already have years of knowledge accumulated on this topic that can help someone who is just starting out and would like to know what you know without having to go through a long learning curve like you did.

Is there enough information online or on books on this topic that I can find easily?

This question goes both ways. Even if you know enough about a topic to write a whole book about it, there are some subjects you might have to investigate a little bit to corroborate that you're right or to prove someone else's point wrong.

If there is too much information that's extremely easy to find then it wouldn't make sense to put even more information out there unless you have a unique angle. Likewise, if there's just too much information out there on the topic, you could find a way to synthesize the most important points and sources in order to save the reader the time to go through all of the free information available.

Is this something I could think, breath and dream about for 30 days without getting tired of it?

This book is about writing a book fast and getting it out there so in order to do so you need to submerge yourself in whatever theme you chose. Are you ready to become an expert on the subject? Because for the next 30 days, the only thing you will be thinking about will be your book.

Now that you're clear on what topic you want and all those little details you need to clear before you start it is time to move on to how you're actually going to write this book. Depending on the length of your book, this part is mostly psychological as you will have to spend more than a few hours per week writing and editing content.

LAYOUT, TIMELINES & CHARACTERS

You are going to need a blueprint of how the book is going to be written. What I do is that I start with the table of content and start writing the names of the chapters as topics I'd like to include in the book. When writing fiction, these chapters can be special or defining events that will happen in the book.

Pick clear titles for every topic that summarize the information you're going to include in each chapter. En example would be to name your chapter "Keto Diet recipes under 10 minutes" rather than "High protein recipes" since it tells the reader exactly what they can find if they go to that chapter. If you're writing a fiction book, these titles should summarize a highlight that's going to happen in the chapter. Titles such as "heartbroken again" are more emotional and connect with the reader better than "December 10 - afternoon". Overall, look for a summary that evokes emotion.

When it comes to picking what each chapter is going to be about (pre-writing) you can brainstorm it on a sheet of paper or even use post its with different colors ideas in each of them and then rearrange them so that you have the main idea/chapter title on top and then many post it notes grouped with the different subtopics underneath.

I like brainstorming because it lets me look at all my ideas in an unorganized way, everything is possible at this point. All the ideas are valid and most of them aren't going to make it to the final edition, so it doesn't matter what you come up with. It is a non-pressuring scenario that allows you to be as creative as you want. The more ideas you have, the easiest it is to keep only the best ones.

This is also a great moment to figure out what you really want to keep in the book and if there are any chapters that you'd rather cut out. You could even find out that perhaps you have enough material to write 3 books instead of 1!

The layout of the fiction book is going to be a little more complicated than that but still doable. There's a step to take previous to start dividing the chapters and it is to establish a time line. This is *essential* for a fiction book and I cannot stress this enough. This will help you understand when everything is happening and if it makes sense for your characters to do something specific according to what was going on with their lives at the time. For example, if your character is studying at university and you want her to take a trip to Europe for a month, it wouldn't make sense for her to take it in February or September. She would most likely be traveling in December or June.

This also helps the reader because if there's a significant jump in time, you can clearly specify how long it's been since that event or how long it's going to be until that event happens.

Depending on when your book is taking place, you might want to divide it into days, months, years or important events. Regardless of how long your timeline is, you will need to correctly identify when each event is going to happen. You can do this by making a simple timeline on a sheet of paper and start adding events. This can be done for each character so that it's easier to notice when, where and how their story connects. This will make it easier for you to write the book as, even if the character is having a flashback to a previous event, you'll know exactly when it was and how it's going to interconnect with other relevant characters' lives.

Think of the characters as real people. They all have different lives, aspirations and fears which will guide their actions in the book. For each character you should write a profile, no longer than one page, to help you identify this faster and keep track of who everyone is. If your most adventurous character is nervous about bungee jumping then there must be a reason behind that. Perhaps he is afraid of heights or had a bad experience when he was younger.

Throughout the book you will notice that sometimes, the characters themselves start changing depending on how the story evolves. It feels just as if it were these fictional characters the ones who were writing the book and you're just here to tell the story. Connect with your characters and do your best to understand them at a deeper level.

On the next page I included an example of what you can include in a profile page. Feel free to add or take anything you consider relevant and have fun with it. Remember you are making a character come to life.

Bonus tip: print this page or have it on hand when you're writing and make sure to include how the characters mutate throughout the story and why.

CHARACTER PROFILE

Name:

Age:

Height:

Weight:

Skin color:

Hair color:

Eye color:

Personality:

Nationality:

Living in:

Occupation:

Degrees:

Achievements:

Style:

Hobbies:

Strengths:

Weaknesses:

Usual phrases:

Biggest dream:

Biggest fear:

Related to & how:

LENGTH

You need to decide how long you want your book to be. If you're writing a non fiction book, it is recommended that it is at least 10,000 as anything less than that might make the book look more like a pamphlet and people will most likely leave negative reviews if it's too short (or overpriced). If you want to write a fiction book, however, you should be aiming for around 50,000 words. Fiction book readers usually consume a lot more material and are more likely to buy a sequel if they liked the story or fell in love with one of the characters. On the other hand, non-fiction readers are searching to find a solution to a particular problem or educate themselves on a particular topic, meaning they will most likely read material that's on the same topic or helps them solve a particular problem they're faced with.

The topic will also dictate how long your book is going to be. If you chose a topic with a lot of information available and you also know a lot about it then it's going to be extremely easy for you to write a long book. Be careful if you're writing a non-fiction book though, as in this case you need to discriminate the information that might not be useful for your reader, as they're usually reading the book to solve a problem they have or to acquire more knowledge. It is different to write a book on cancer research (which might need to be longer in order to thoroughly explain all of the subjects) than it is to write it on how to write a book or start a Youtube channel. Even within fiction books there are some which are on the short side (20,000 words) and some that are on the longer side (150,000 words). If your story is so good it needs to be written in 150k words then you can always divide it into 3 shorter books and make it a saga.

Knowing the length of the book is going to be extremely helpful to stay consistent, which is what we're going to talk about in the next chapter. Since our goal with this book is to help you write your book in one month, you should use this number and divide it into 20. So if your goal is to write a 30,000 word book, you should aim to write 1,500 words per day. If you want to write a 50,000 words book then you should be aiming for 2,500 words per day. You might be asking yourself, why is she dividing it by 20 if there's 30 days in a month? And the answer is as simple as the question: you're not going to write 2,500 words every single day. Life gets in the way and some days it seems there isn't enough time to even sleep 5 hours. Don't worry, I got you covered. This is the reason why you'll be dividing your goal length into 20, these are the total days you're most likely be hitting your goal and then you don't need to worry if you only write half of your goal one day as you have enough room to finish it the next day. It also gives you enough time to send the book for editing, formatting and order a cover or design it yourself.

One more thing, if you have a fiction book that's over 200,000 words or a non-fiction book that's over 100,000 you might want to consider dividing it into two volumes instead of having a massive book that people are afraid to even start reading. If you are a new author, your book should be in that sweet spot in which it is long enough to be inviting and "worth the price" but short enough so that people actually want to read it and not think it's going to take them a lifetime to finish.

CONSISTENCY IS KEY

You might think that you can write 5,000 words in one day because you've done so previously for an essay you had to hand in for university the next day. Truth is, if you want to finish your book it is best to divide the task into a certain number of words you commit to writing everyday. It is a lot better (and doable) to write 2,000 words per day and do it consistently than to try to write 5,000 per day, every single day and fail miserably because it's hard even for an experienced writer to write 5,000 words per day. In my personal experience I have found that I can write 2,000 words consistently without burning out or getting tired of the book and up to 4,000 in a day if I have to skip a day of writing for whatever reason. Your own range depends on how used you are to writing and how much you have to say. If you find that you can only write 1,000 words per day consistently then stick to doing so but keep in mind that it's going to take you twice the time than it'd take you if you were writing 2,000 words per day. The difference between those who can publish a book in one month and those who can't is consistency.

Be realistic about how much time you can dedicate to your book per day and then make a commitment to do so. There are going to be distractions, very tempting nights out with friends and even an article on psoriasis is going to become the most interesting article in the world in order to procrastinate in the writing of your book. Do not cave in for these distractions. Your own brain is going to try to sabotage you and distract you with other activities and you might even get anxiety thinking your book isn't "good enough" before it's even written and find every excuse in order to postpone it. Can you see the irony? If anything, you can publish the book under a pen name so that the criticisms don't feel that harsh.

Make writing a habit, it doesn't matter at what time you choose to write. You can commit to writing everyday at 10 am after breakfast or at 9 pm after you've come back from the gym and showered. The time you'll be using to write is going to depend on your own schedule and lifestyle. When are you most creative? In the morning or at night?

Right after you've woken up or when you just got back from the gym? It doesn't matter when you choose to write as long as you write for at least one hour everyday. Pick the time you will be writing beforehand and then try to stick to it. Creating the habit of writing will make it 10 times easier for you to write faster and blocking the time mentally will prepare you to power through the writing. In the end, "it's only for one hour".

When it comes to writing, just write. Write whatever comes to your head about the topic and keep writing. Do not stop to edit as this can cut your creative flow. Just keep writing and eventually, something good will come out and you won't even believe you wrote such a masterpiece looking back.

Also, if you are one of those kamikaze types that can write 12,000 words in one day and would rather be done in 24 hours this is also valid. You could take a whole weekend to lock yourself in your room and write like a maniac for 3 days to come out with the finished product. You are the one who will decide how and when it's done, just make sure you are consistent until you finish.

Whether it is 20 days with 2,000 words or 3 days with 6,000 words, keep going until you are done and don't take more than one day of rest in between writing days. Yes, you should even write during weekends and weekdays after work. In the best case scenario, you should be writing everyday, even if it's a few hundred words. The key here is to know yourself and which type of writing you prefer.

If you are not feeling like writing at all just write one sentence. That's it, turn on your computer, open the file and write one sentence. This will most likely have a snowball effect in which you'll start writing about other topics and even be able to complete a chapter or a few. The first step is always the hardest and I understand that somedays, motivation is just not there and you shouldn't expect it to be there throughout the month. This is why it is so important to have a clear reason why you want (and need) to finish this book in a month. Maybe you want to write it before your 25th birthday or need to publish it before a specific deadline such as Amazon Prime Day in order to sell 4x the amount of copies you'd sell on any other day, let this be your motivator when everything else fails and hold on to it like it's your warhorse.

I once went to a job interview in which the interviewer asked me what I did for work and I told him I was a writer and had written a few books. What I found interesting is that he then proceeded to ask where I found the inspiration to write the books. I answered that I found that discipline usually precedes inspiration, and that it is a lot easier to get inspired if you commit to sitting down and writing even when nothing's coming out. He probably thought I was a psycho, but I got offered that job. Everything about my answer was totally true though, whatever activity it is that I decide to start, the same story repeats itself. When you sit down and dedicate a set amount of time to whatever it is you're doing, it will be a lot easier to get inspired and finish the project instead of passively staring at it from a distance and waiting months to get inspired to continue writing.

ACTUAL WRITING

Where should you start? The answer? Anywhere and everywhere, as long as you start it doesn't really matter much where. I usually start with whatever chapter captures my attention the most so that I can be super excited and start on a good note. Then, if a random idea pops into my mind about a paragraph I could add to another chapter, I just go straight to it and start writing. Some writers prefer to start on the first chapter and then continue until they're done with the last one. If you have no idea where to start, you can always write the names of the chapters on a piece of paper, fold them and then pick one randomly. Even if you have nothing to write, it will be a clear sign that you need to start investigating that topic and dedicating it more time so that you can go through it easily.

I get that it can be overwhelming to have such a big project ahead but think about it this way, every word you write will bring you closer to the finishing line so the sooner you start, the sooner you'll be done. Also, the more you write, the faster you'll finish. Even if you can only bring yourself to write 100 words one day, you will still be 100 words closer to a finished book.

Do not procrastinate. Start as soon as possible and write as much as you can, even if you're not sure you're going to include the material. Ideas about what to write usually sneak up on you in the worst places and when this happens you need to be prepared. If you come up with ideas while you're in the bathroom/bus/bar then be it and send yourself a text message with whatever you came up with. If you tell yourself you're just going to write about it when you get home, it is most likely going to slip through your fingers and you'll forget as soon as you're back in a comfortable writing place. If you have something to add, do it now.

Once you have those few paragraphs, you need to accept that it's not going to be perfect. You need to let go of the idea that your first book is going to be perfect, even if that's the only thing you want from it. Don't criticize yourself too hard or too fast as the first material you'll write is probably not going to be your favorite. Give it a few days before you start editing and then delete or edit it if it's that bad. Finished is better than perfect and from my experience, it will never be "perfect" in your eyes. Now, even though it might not be perfect, this doesn't give you an excuse to just publish whatever comes to your mind. Of course you can't expect to publish a crappy book and then expect it to sell, bad reviews will probably kill it before it gets far enough.

MINDSET

Instead of saying stuff like "Oh, I can't write a book because _____" start setting yourself up for success with reasons and actions that will show you why you can write a book. Perhaps you are knowledgeable on the topic or are good at researching so you can find all of the information online. It doesn't matter as long as you are your own cheerleader or just the one who will make you resort to pure discipline when it comes to writing when you don't feel like doing it at all.

Your mindset is usually influenced heavily by the people you surround yourself with. Pay attention to how the people around you react when you tell them about your projects. Are they supportive and encouraging, doubt you will be able to do it or just criticizing everything you do? Sometimes we just need someone to give us a few encouraging words so that we can find extra motivation to finish our books. Know who these supportive people are and seek their guidance when the path gets rough and you want to quit. Don't forget to thank them for all of their help and time as these people are probably worth keeping around and try being supportive to them as well when they need you.

Life advice: those who do not support you and do not get happy for your achievements aren't your real friends. Find people who you can trust and talk about your dreams and ideas with.

I believe you can do this and whoever says otherwise is lying! You wouldn't be reading a book on how to do it if you weren't committed enough. If you do not have a support system where you live then you can always join Facebook groups with other authors. There's a whole community of people who give advice to others and love to help. Remember you're not alone in this journey and finding a mentor might be easier than you think. Now that you have answered the how, it is time to put in the action to make your book a reality.

Having said that, your worst enemies aren't going to be those criticizing your book, it is going to be yourself. It is going to feel as if it's a massive task you can't complete and you're going to want to quit at least 10 times. Keep going. Breaking it down will make it a more achievable task in your head. Think of the book in smaller units, a chapter is not as intimidating as a whole book so instead of thinking of it as "I have to write a book this month" think about it like "I have to write a chapter today/this weekend". Even if a chapter seems too daunting you just need to remember that a chapter is a group of paragraphs, which is a bunch of sentences. One sentence feels like nothing but it's going to bring you closer to the finishing line.

NEW MATERIAL

You've now written around 8,000 words, you're halfway through the book you've always wanted to write but there's a little problem... you've ran out of inspiration. Literally nothing is coming out of your head, no matter how hard you try. Instead of staring blankly at the page with nothing else to write, start investigating and getting inspired.

There is plenty of information on the subject and it's available in any format you might want it: video, audio or text. If you're writing a book on makeup, just go to Google or Youtube and search the specific topic you're looking for. Even searching for "edible makeup" is valid and there are almost 22 million results on Google!

Reading articles about the subject you're writing about is going to expand your own knowledge and therefore content by giving you new ideas. This doesn't mean you should be copying other people's work, never do that. It means that they might mention something you hadn't even considered but that it is relevant and that your audience might benefit from. If you're going to include someone else's work in your book, be sure to cite it correctly and give them the credit, it's their work after all.

Watching videos on the topic you're writing about will open you up to other's people views and experiences and it will also give you plenty of visual content to make your book more descriptive. This is specially important if you're writing a fiction book and you want the scenery to be vivid without leaving your cozy house. Watch people's videos or look at photographs of the place and you might even find a new detail you had overlooked.

If you're writing a fiction book that's set on a city you've never been to, don't worry, there are plenty of resources online that you can use to make it seem like you've been there and are familiar with the area. First, is Google maps, in which you can just access the area and even "walk" around as if you were there. This will help you see what the layout looks like and how long it takes to go from place to place. While this might not be a perfect substitute, it's a huge step. You can also watch people's blogs on Youtube which will give you a pretty good idea of how the streets look like on certain seasons. Along with that, you can watch people's experiences when moving to the city or their impressions after having lived there for a year or so.

Talking to other people might also inspire you to write about content you hadn't thought about previously. Different people have different points of view and also different needs. You might be seeing the book from an angle that no one had thought of but you also need to include other angles to tie it with preconceived knowledge. A friend of mine always says that two heads think better than one. You should aim to understand their perspective and then incorporate it into your own material, making your position stronger or easier to understand for others who might think like them.

If you've ran out of content to write, it could also be that you're no longer inspired by the topic of your book or that you're tired of thinking and writing about _____ all day everyday. It might seem like a good idea to rest for two or three days in order to find the love for this topic again. Do not do this. Stay consistent and write every single day if you can, even if it's just 500 words that you're going to delete in the future. Believe me, those 2 days will end up becoming 5 days and then a month and you'll still be on chapter 1 of your beloved (yet unfinished) book.

When everything else fails (or even when everything is going great), try freely writing everything that comes to your mind. While you might end up deleting half of what you wrote, the other half will most likely be amazing or at least insightful. It is preferable to look back at a page filled with spelling mistakes and sentences that don't really make sense (yet!) than it is to come back to a blank page. You can at least work with errors but you can't work with nothing.

While writing and editing your book you also need to ask yourself if the content you're providing is valuable to your reader. If you could've said the same thing in 10,000 words than in 100,000 words then you'd be making yourself and your reader a favor by saving you both 90% of your time. A longer book doesn't necessarily mean a better book. This goes to readers as well, it is preferable to read a book filled with value that can be finished in an hour than it is to read one with a lot of filling that's going to take you 5. Focus on the value you're creating for the reader and keep being valuable a top priority, specially if your name is going to be featured on your book as it is a lot harder to come back from an awful book than to start with a clean slate. (Unless it goes viral for how bad it is.)

LOGISTICS OF BOOK WRITING

Now, we've covered content, let's talk logistics. Obviously you're going to need a place in which to write your book. Some people prefer to write it on paper, some on their computer. Choose the computer from the start and get used to writing there. This will save you a lot of time and money if you don't want to pay someone to transcript your writing or if you don't have the time to do it yourself.

When it comes to where you should be writing the book, I personally use Pages and keep a copy on Google Docs. You can use Words and save it on a USB, just make sure you have a backup in case you a) lose your computer, b) lose the USB, c) accidentally delete the file, etc.

Even if you decide to use Word or Pages to write your book, I would suggest you keep notes on your phone or a Document on Google Docs with ideas for your book. Sometimes we get amazing ideas while we're driving or far away from our computers and it is essential that you write them down before you forget. Having your phone nearby will help you keep track of these great ideas as you can add them to the book document, your notes or even send yourself a voice note on WhatsApp talking about what you plan to write next. I like using Google Docs as I can keep the ideas for different books separated and in order so that when I want to start writing and I've run out of ideas I can just go in and take one of the paragraphs I wrote while at the gym.

Sometimes we get these moments of brilliance while doing a completely random activity, this is because the information has been circling our subconscious and something has been created without us noticing. This is one of the reasons why it is important to write about something you're passionate or curious about, you need to be prepared to have your whole mind invaded by this topic throughout a whole month. While is another reason why you should power through your book writing, once it is done, it's done. If you casually write 1 chapter every two months, the book will take forever to finish and it'll be a lot harder to keep track of what's going on and to tie together the different topics.

When it comes to writing the book you, once again, need to find what works best for you. I write my books on a single Pages document from start to finish and just add and edit as I go. I watched a video from a girl who preferred to write each chapter individually on one document. I like to jump from chapter to chapter and add information to each one as I think about it but if you'd rather have it separated in blocks that you focus on and tackle that subject then that's up to you. Following a certain writing preference doesn't mean you can't switch or mix them. Initially you're going to want to experiment with this until you find your perfect balance.

WRITING AS A BUSINESS

If you plan to write in order to make money you first need to test the demand. If you want to write a book on how to make thumbnails for Youtube but no one is searching for that then the book is not going to sell, plain and simple. So, the first step should be to look for a topic that's going to sell before you even start writing your book.

Also, if writing is an activity you dislike, there is no need to write your own book. You can still share your knowledge with the world by hiring a ghostwriter and working together in the process or you could use the dictate tool on your phone and just talk. There are plenty of options if you want to publish a book and thanks to technology you don't even need to write it yourself. If you would like to hire someone to help you with the writing then there are plenty of companies that provide this service. You can find them online, as well as freelancers, by searching for writers on Google or Fiverr. Make sure to check the ratings and reviews as not all of them are good. This includes both freelancers as well as companies but usually companies only hire writers who prove that they have the skills to write a book.

For me, this was one of the most challenging steps as there are many people offering ghostwriting services but a lot of them aren't good writers. Usually, if they're "too good to be true" they're probably not good writers and are plagiarizing content from somewhere. I had one of my freelance writers plagiarize almost an entire book and then sell it to me as if he had written it. It was re-structured in such a way that most websites to check plagiarized content couldn't detect it. This is very dangerous from a legal standpoint as this was a copyrighted work from another person. Obviously I didn't end up publishing it and I never hired this freelancer again but it makes me think that if I hadn't checked three times in different websites and through different methods I could've gotten into a lot of (expensive legal) trouble. So the lesson here is: hire a trustworthy company or writer and check twice that the content wasn't stolen from another book or article.

Also, don't just publish content that's public domain. This is a lazy move and your readers will soon realize that they could've found all of the information online for free.

I would strongly suggest you use a writing company rather than a freelancer for this step as this offers you an extra layer of protection. Now, moving on from the writing process, what do you do when you want to translate a book you already wrote? This is a whole different scenario as this content is already created by you. Meaning, you own the rights and should have no problem translating it into another language or into 10 languages and publishing it.

One way to expand your brand and get to more people in markets with less competition is to translate your book into another language. Before doing this you should also test the demand on those markets to see if it's worth your time or money to translate this book. There are topics which are super famous in english speaking markets but that when translated into Spanish they generate no sales. Different people have different interests and these vary even more when you look at them from different cultures. One very clear example is Minimalism, while this might be a huge topic in the US between some groups of people, I have a few Latin American friends who had never heard of it and even asked what minimalism was. Needless to say, they weren't particularly interested in becoming minimalists or reading a book on minimalism. While this might not be the best example, just by going to Amazon and searching for minimalism (and the equivalent translation in other languages) you will see in the amount of books published on this topic as well as the reviews on each book that it's nowhere near as popular.

CROSS PLATFORM MONETIZATION

If you're going to write (or publish) as a way to make more money, I suppose that you're also looking for other ways to maximize your earnings. A great way to use your content and effort more than once is to use what you publish on a blog or vice versa. One or two articles from your blog could be a chapter from your book and it is a lot easier to write a book if you already have part of the material and knowledge on the topic. Having a blog is also going to keep your ideas organized by topic and title, even if you're not planning to write a book on a particular article that you've posted you can still use a lot of the content to do add to other chapters or include as some sort of subchapter. This also works the other way around, you can use your book and divide it into blog posts that you post every week or so and you can even use them as special content for your subscribers.

The monetization of your book doesn't end in publishing, it begins. There are many ways besides written content to help you expand your brand. Here I will include some examples:

- Make a Youtube video about one of your chapters and leave the link to your book in the description. Youtube income doesn't only come from views, it also puts you in front of a bigger audience so that your book can become known by people outside of your blog or Amazon. On top of that, you can also monetize your views on Youtube once you get to 1,000 subscribers and have another stream of income. The benefit of starting a Youtube channel is that you don't need a huge investment to start. It is free to register and you can use your phone's camera to film. However, you might need to invest in an editing software or invest time to learn how to use the editing software. Other costs include a tripod and lights.

- Start a podcast in which you talk about the topics you included in your book. Once again, you could use every chapter as an episode for your podcast. This puts you in front of podcast listeners who might be interested in your topic. If this becomes popular then you can also make more money from your book by including an audio version and including it on audible.

- Launch your own course using the ideas you taught in your book. A course is a great way to generate passive income while also helping people learn a valuable skill. However, it will probably require a lot of time up front to build it as well as some time to market it so that it can be an evergreen source of income.

- Create an infographic to post on Instagram and leave a link to your book on your profile. This will reach people interested in the topic you wrote about if you tag it properly. Remember to add value to the people who look at your posts.

LEGAL

Of course a huge part of publishing as a business is the legal side. You do not want to be held accountable for the results of your audience, specially if they end up losing money. The best thing you can do in order to protect yourself from any liabilities is to hire a lawyer to write a disclaimer for your book. This usually doesn't happen but it is best if you're protected from the start.

It's also very important to invest in copyrighting as you will want to protect your content from being used by other people who claim it as theirs. Copyright laws and other laws vary depending on the country and even the state or city you're in. However, there is a common area that guides how these laws are structured in most places. Principles such as the protection of the author as well as the customer can be found in most.

Remember not to take content from any other author as you may be violating copyright laws.

BEFORE PUBLISHING

Before you consider publishing your book there are a few steps you should take to make sure everything is in order.

Edit

Go through your book and start editing those bits that don't make sense or that could be expressed differently for easier understanding.

Proofread

It is not uncommon to have grammar or spelling mistakes, specially if you've just written a whole book in under one month. Re read the whole thing and ask someone else to read it as well and give you feedback. You can also hire a freelancer to help you with proofreading. Make sure that the person you hire has good reviews and previous experience. Make sure there are no spelling mistakes or typos that could've been omitted.

Send it to a friend

Sometimes, opinions of our friends are very valuable and they can spot mistakes that we didn't notice. Don't let this set you back too long if this friend doesn't read the book in two weeks. Express clearly that you would like some feedback as soon as he or she has time to read the book and send you some suggestions.

Cover

Order a cover or make a cover yourself that looks professional. If you're unsure about a particular freelancer or what you would like to include in your cover, you can order a few different ones from different freelancers to make sure you get exactly what you want. Make sure the title and subtitle are easy to read and that the cover catches the eyes of potential customers. Remember that your cover is the first contact with the client and it can either work wonders or end up being ignored...resulting in no sales. If you'd like to make the cover yourself, there are some beautiful stock images on **unsplash.com** which you can download and use for free. The one I used for this cover was by **Alif Caesar Rizqi Pratama** on **Unsplash**.

Description

If you're publishing on Amazon or any other site that features a space to write a description about your book, make sure you write one that will sell. You have already caught the attention of the customer with your cover, the description should give that last push so that he or she buys the book.

Keywords

Keywords are the words that people type into the search bar in order to find your book. These are extremely important because the reader wants to be able to find your book under the right keyword or keywords. If your book is about turtles, do not write "lion" as a keyword. You can add "turtle", "marine life", "sea animals", etc, you get the idea. You can make your keywords more efficient by using Amazon's search bar to look at the suggestions it shows. These will appear right below the search bar and will give you suggestions on how to complete the term you're searching for.

Formatting

This is a fairly easy step to do if you know how to do it. If not, you can watch tutorials on Youtube as there are plenty and they can explain it to you 10 times better than I ever could through a book. Basically all you'll need is Word and basic knowledge on how to use it, everything else you can learn from a tutorial. Personally I prefer to hire a freelancer to format my books as it's faster and very cheap. Freelancers shouldn't charge you more than $5 for a 100 page book unless you have too many illustrations. If you'd like to hire a freelancer I suggest you look for one in **Fiverr** as they offer many amazing and useful services.

This is pretty much everything you need to check and do before publishing. If you have a set date to publish your book I suggest you take into consideration that this whole process of proofreading and editing might take you around a week.

PUBLISHING DOESN'T NEED TO BE HARD

Publishing is by far the easiest step of the whole process. It is free, takes only an hour to set up your account and the hardest part is to pick the category as there are plenty to choose from. This is if you're going to publish your book on Amazon KDP, which is why I recommend starting here.

Personally, if it wasn't for Amazon KDP I don't think I would have been able to publish my books as fast or easily as I did. Most publishers in my country make writers hire specific proofreaders and then reject 9 out of 10 books that authors want to publish. Publishing on KDP is free, which means it removes the risk (economically speaking) for you as a writer as well as for a publishing company that would've had to incur in extra costs to make your book a reality.

Within Amazon KDP there are a few steps which you'll need to take. The first one is to register with your email and a password, then you'll have to fill out a tax form and choose a payment method.

Once you've been through all of this then you can start publishing. Let's go through all of the process you need to go through when publishing.

The first thing to do is to go into Amazon KDP, this is as easy as typing Amazon KDP on Google or going to their website which is **kdp.amazon.com** . Once you're in you log in or create your account, fill out the tax info and all that jazz.

Here comes the interesting part! You're going to go into **Bookshelf > Create a New Title > + Kindle Ebook**. This should take you into a page that says **Kindle eBook Details**.

Language

Select the language your book's in. It's most likely going to be in English so you can go ahead and select that one.

Book Title

This one is important, your book title should be interesting and give the reader an idea of what to expect when he or she reads your book. Of course, you can't make a title too long or it's going to be hard to remember and to fit into your cover. So what do you do then if you can't fit everything you want the reader to know into the title? You use the subtitle to give additional details! One example could be: Title: Cooking Guide for Single Moms. Subtitle: The easiest and fastest recipes for those moms who value their time and their family. What this is going to do is that it'll make the title look more appealing but it will also help your book rank when single moms search it on the search bar.

Series

Are you planning to write a series of books? Then it would be ideal to have a name for the series as well as an idea of where this book is going to fit within it. Is this the first book of the series or the last one?

Edition Number

If this is your first book you can leave this blank.

Author

This is your time! Add your name or pen name here so that readers can look for your content that way.

Contributors

Did you co-write this book with someone else like a friend or a coworker? It would be a wonderful idea to add their name! Otherwise, this can be left blank. If you hired a ghostwriter you can also leave this blank.

Description

Ok, I don't want to scare you but this is one of the most important parts of book publishing. You *need* a good description. Think of it this way, people are going to look at your super cool cover, read the title and think "this is exactly what I need!" and then go into your book's page. If the description is like "yeah, this is an alright book" then that's going to discourage the customer from buying your book. The description should *scream* "this is the best book you'll read and this is why you need it!"

Publishing Rights

Basically this is asking you if you wrote this book or if you copy-pasted it from the internet. Select "I own the copyright and I hold the necessary publishing rights." if you wrote this book or hired someone else to do it and then bought the rights for it. I'd like to stress the importance of not copying material from someone else as they could sue you for stealing their intellectual property. This is the reason why we can't just copy-paste a book and then publish as our own. This is also what's going to protect you from someone else stealing your book and publishing it as their own.

Keywords

Another super important factor to take into consideration are keywords. These are going to help the reader find your book. Keywords are those strings of words you search in the search bar in order to find what you want to read or buy. Going back to the example, if your book is a cooking book for single moms you should add keywords such as "cooking book", "cooking for kids", "fast and healthy recipes" etc. Amazon lets you add up to 7 keywords, I suggest you use all 7 of them.

Categories

Categories are also going to help the reader find your book, if your book is fiction, don't list it under romance. I'd suggest you take some time to go through all the categories your book could fit into and then pick the best two that you think are going to get to your target audience the easiest.

Age and Range

This is important if you're writing a children's book or an adult's book. If you wrote a book for kids in Kindergarten, the best idea would be to set the range for kids around those ages. If your book contains mature content, the best idea would be to set it at 18+ for age range.

Pre-Order

I would suggest you don't use this option yet as you don't know if you'll be able to finish your book before the designated time. If you fail to deliver your book on the date you set, you will lose your privileges to set it to pre-order.

We are now done with Kindle eBook Details! How are you doing so far? All good? Alright, select Save and Continue and let's move on to **Kindle eBook Content**.

Manuscript

Here you can choose if you enable Digital Rights Management or not. Personally I don't have it enabled but it is meant to protect your book from unauthorized distribution.

The time has come to upload the manuscript of your book. This can be in a lot of different formats including .doc, .docx, HTML, MOBI, ePub, RTF, Plain Text, and KPF. I personally upload all of mine in MOBI since I've found it to be friendly and easy to upload. I couldn't give you more information on the other formats as I've uploaded my books in MOBI since I started publishing. This step might take a while so don't worry if it takes like 7 minutes, your book might be very heavy or your internet speed might be slow. If this is taking too long, you can refresh the page and try again. Once it is uploaded successfully, it will say "Manuscript "titleofthebook" uploaded successfully!" and it will also let you know if it has any spelling errors that you might want to check.

Kindle eBook Cover

Next up is the cover. Covers are important, don't try to save a few bucks and then end up with a horrible cover. If you don't know how to design covers, it's better to leave it to the freelancers with good reviews. Once you have your cover you can upload it here, it should be in JPG format (or TIFF) because otherwise it won't let you upload it. Once it has been uploaded, it should say "cover uploaded successfully".

Kindle eBook Preview

I would suggest you do launch the previewer just to make sure everything looks fine. If the text or cover is not centered or it just doesn't look good, make sure to edit it before publishing.

Kindle eBook ISBN

This is a number that's assigned to your book when you publish, you can leave this space blank unless you already have an ISBN.

Not so hard to publish a book huh? We're now on the final step before publishing. Click Save and Continue and we will look into the **Kindle eBook Pricing**.

KDP Select Enrollment

Enrolling in this is like being "exclusive" with Amazon. So you will have your book only in Amazon KDP for 3 months. I usually select this option as I don't have my books anywhere else, however if you want to have your own store or sell them through other publishers you won't be able to have this option. This is useful as it lets you run promotions from time to time.

Territories

Do you want your book to be available worldwide or just in a few selected territories? I selected Worldwide but you can choose any of them if you only hold rights in an individual territory or if you don't want your book to be available outside the U.S. for example.

Royalty and Pricing

Here you can select how much royalties you want to receive for each copy sold. It can be either 35% or 70% and it depends on the price of your ebook. If it's between $2.99 and $9.99 then you can earn 70% royalty. Once you choose the price of your book you can automatically match it in other markets (€2.99) with other currencies or choose a different price on other markets (€2.50).

Matchbook

If you have a paperback version of the book, people who bought it can have access to your ebook for a lower price or even for free. I have this option enabled as they have already paid for the book so it makes sense to give the ebook as well so that readers can have it accesible everywhere they go.

Book Lending

You can choose to allow your book being lended to other people by readers (if they've already purchased it) for 14 days.

Terms and Conditions

The terms and conditions you agree to once you publish the book. You can read more by clicking the link they provide.

Once you've been through all of these steps, your book is finally ready to be published so just click on "**Publish your Kindle eBook**" and your book should be available soon.

Pretty simple right? Don't worry if you still don't understand some of the categories, it takes time to get used to all of them but the more you publish, the easier it will be.

Now that you know how to publish an eBook we can go through the process of how to publish a paperback. It is pretty much the same so I'm just going to add the parts in which it's different. The first page (**Paperback Details**) will be pretty much the same so let's go ahead and look at the differences with the middle section, "**Paperback Content**".

Print ISBN

So the first step here is to get assigned an ISBN as all books have one. You can just click on "assign me a free KDP ISBN" and you'll be assigned one immediately.

Publication Date

Here you can choose the date in which you first published your book or you can just leave it black and it'll auto-fill with the date in which it's published.

Print Options

Here's one of the parts in which it changes the most compared to the eBook. You will be given the option to choose the interior and paper type, trim size, bleed settings and paperback cover finish so let's go through each one of the.

Interior and Paper Type: Here you can choose to have it in black and white or color with white or cream paper. I personally choose black and white ink with white paper because I mostly publish non-fiction books. If you're going to publish fiction books, the cream paper is probably the best option as it's easier on the eyes and since customers are going to be reading the book for a long time this could help them a lot.

Trim size: This is the size of your book, there are many options such as 5"x8", 6"x9", etc. Choose the one you think it's going to go best with your book. Your book will need to be in this size but you can download the template for the book directly through Amazon.

Bleed settings: "bleed" allows printing at or off the end of a page and it's usually used for books with illustrations. I always choose "no bleed" but if you're publishing a children's book with whole pages of illustrations you might want to check how this works.

Paperback cover finish: You can choose if it's matte or glossy.

Manuscript

You will need to upload your manuscript in PDF, remember this has to be in the size that you chose for trim size so the actual document has to be in that specific size. If you don't know how to set your document on 5" by 8" you can just download a template from Amazon. My two go-to sizes are 5 x 8 and 6 x 9 so I just download and save the template and then when I'm ready to publish I just adjust it and export to PDF.

Book Cover

Ok, this part is a little tricky if you are designing your cover or using the one you used for the eBook as this cover includes the back and spine of the book. If you only have the ebook cover then you can use the cover creator and finish the back and spine yourself. This process isn't complicated at all but if you don't feel comfortable doing it you can just hire a freelancer to help you with it and design a cover with a spine and back for you to upload it directly.

Book Preview

Here's where you check if your formatting and cover look good. I would strongly suggest you launch the previewer and really take the time to make sure everything is okay.

Now we can move on to **Paperback Rights and Pricing**. This is pretty similar to the one we went through with the ebook with the exception that it's going to give you a minimum price you can give to your book. Why? Because it costs money to print it so Amazon calculates a price which works for you both. In here you can get 60% royalties and then if you choose to have expanded distribution (which sells the book through other retailers) you get 40%.

That's pretty much it and if you completed all of the steps you should've pretty much published your books in around 24 hours (depending on when you clicked publish).

RESOURCES

Freelancers

For freelancer, I usually hire people from **Fiverr**. Whenever I need a cover, proofreading or formatting help I just go to their website and search for someone offering the service I'm looking for.

Amazon KDP

Publish your own books for free on Amazon's **Kindle Direct Publishing**.

Getting Paid

If you live in the United States, you will most likely get a cheque from Amazon or a Direct Deposit. However, if you live outside of the US and you need a method to receive your payments you can use **Payoneer**. Make sure that **Payoneer** operates in your country and it's possible for you to create your account with them. By using my link, we both get $25* when you sign up.

If you need any help with setting up your account with Amazon KDP, you can search for pretty much anything on Youtube. Even when you get to the part in which you need to put in your tax information.

Youtube

Here you can find video tutorials on how to do pretty much everything. If you don't understand a step or would like to see how the platform looks you can search for a tutorial on the topic.

SUMMARY

I'm one of those people who value their time basically over everything else. I am sure you're also a pretty busy person yourself so here I condensed all the lessons of the book into two pages so that you can easily read the summary and get the information you need.

When writing a book, it is important to find who your target market is so that you can tailor the content to them in order to increase sales. Once you're writing the book there are many techniques you can follow but the most important part is that you learn how you work best so that you can write your book more efficiently. If you work better at 10 pm after you come back home from work, then write then but if you write better right after waking up then that should be the window you use to write. Remember to write consistently and everyday if you want better results as you might find yourself slipping if you skip a day of writing and then the book just becomes an unfinished project buried in folders on your computer that you never look at. If you don't like writing you can use the tool dictate or even hire a freelancer to write it for you or to transcript your voice recordings.

In order to write your book you can use different platforms such as Pages, Word or even Google Docs. Whatever you decide to use, I would suggest you keep the original as well as a copy on a USB or online just in case you accidentally delete the file or lose your computer.

Once you have your book ready I would recommend you edit, proofread and send it for formatting. While it's being edited you can either design the cover yourself or hire a freelancer to do it for you. Remember the cover is what's going to catch the customer's eye so you want it to be perfect. Once you have the book and cover ready you can format it yourself or send it for formatting which will cost around $5 for 100 pages. You want it to be converted to MOBI format or any other format that's accepted by Amazon KDP.

Once your book is ready you can go into Amazon KDP to sign up and starting uploading your own books. This process is relatively easy but you will also need to fill out a tax form. Remember that taxes are not something to play with so please take your time and make sure all of the information is correct. Once your account is ready you can publish your book by going into Bookshelf > Create a New Title > Kindle eBook / Paperback. Once you go through the steps here you can Publish your book and it should be available to the public in a few days.

ABOUT THE AUTHOR

Hello! My name is Isabella for those of you who don't know me. I have my own publishing business which I started in 2017 and it has been growing consistently every month. As I started gaining more confidence to tell people what I did and self proclaimed myself as a writer I noticed that one of the most common answers and reactions was that they also wanted to write a book but couldn't for some reason. I personally believe that writing a book or having a blog is a great way to share your knowledge with the world and that if you have something worth sharing then it should be your duty to share it with the people who want to listen.

The first book I wrote was around 10,000 words and it took me months to finish. It didn't matter what I did or what I changed, the book always seemed incomplete. Learning to let go of the belief that everything needs to be perfect is extremely difficult but necessary if you want to succeed as you will have to step out of your comfort zone. The good news is that the more you step out of it, the easier it is and the bigger it gets. The end result?: a more confident you. Also, one very exciting upside I found was that you can actually make money from publishing. Which means you don't need to be approved by a publishing company or sell your soul to start earning a living from doing something you absolutely love. Therefore, if writing is what you love doing, I encourage you to start and work on your first book until it's finished and then publish it, even if you're a bit shy about it. I promise you that it will be one of the best feelings in the world.

Please tell me what you thought of this book by leaving a review. The process of writing books is super extensive so I plan to upload an updated version next year and include everything I learn until then.

If you would like to ask me anything, tell me what you thought about this book or send me feedback on what I could do better or include in the next edition, please send me a message to **isabella_gordillo_@hotmail.com**

Thank you so much for reading this book!

Printed in Great Britain
by Amazon